when all else fails

when all else fails:

poetic wisdom

charles r. ringma

RESOURCE *Publications* • Eugene, Oregon

WHEN ALL ELSE FAILS
Poetic Wisdom

Copyright © 2021 Charles R. Ringma. All rights reserved. Except for brief quotations in critical publications or reviews, no part of this book may be reproduced in any manner without prior written permission from the publisher. Write: Permissions, Wipf and Stock Publishers, 199 W. 8th Ave., Suite 3, Eugene, OR 97401.

Resource Publications
An Imprint of Wipf and Stock Publishers
199 W. 8th Ave., Suite 3
Eugene, OR 97401

www.wipfandstock.com

PAPERBACK ISBN: 978-1-6667-1472-2
HARDCOVER ISBN: 978-1-6667-1473-9
EBOOK ISBN: 978-1-6667-1474-6

SEPTEMBER 7, 2021

for

Paul and Gail Stevens

whose friendship and generosity

knows no bounds.

Contents

PREFACE | xi

achieve | 1
act | 2
agency | 3
answer | 4
anticipation | 5
anxiety | 6
art | 7
beauty | 8
becoming | 9
being | 10
commitment | 11
communion | 12
compromise | 13
consolation | 14
contentment | 15
control | 16
convenience | 17
curiosity | 18
dabble | 19
doubt | 20
duty | 21
energy | 22
enlightenment | 23

envy | 24
faith | 25
fate | 26
fear | 27
fecundity | 28
gaze | 29
gentleness | 30
generosity | 31
gift | 32
gratitude | 33
help | 34
holding | 35
hope | 36
hospitality | 37
hurt | 38
interruption | 39
insight | 40
joy | 41
justice | 42
lament | 43
limitation | 44
listless | 45
liturgy | 46

luminous | 47
maintenance | 48
manifestation | 49
maturity | 50
memory | 51
mending | 52
mentoring | 53
mercy | 54
midwifery | 55
monotone | 56
mourning | 57
mystical | 58
naming | 59
narrators | 60
neighbour | 61
neophyte | 62
nestle | 63
nutritive | 64
occupation | 65
ode | 66
omission | 67
opportunity | 68
orchestrate | 69
ought | 70
outlier | 71
overflow | 72
paradox | 73
pardon | 74
paschal | 75

patience | 76
perseverance | 77
precarious | 78
prelude | 79
provoke | 80
radical | 81
rapine | 82
ready | 83
reciprocity | 84
renew | 85
reprieve | 86
restore | 87
return | 88
risk | 89
routine | 90
sabbath | 91
sacramental | 92
sacrifice | 93
satyagraha | 94
search | 95
shadow | 96
tapestry | 97
tension | 98
test | 99
thankfulness | 100
threshold | 101
trace | 102
transition | 103
twilight | 104

unbearable | 105
uncertain | 106
underestimate | 107
understory | 108
unguarded | 109
unity | 110
unknowing | 111
utopia | 112
verdant | 113
vicarious | 114
visitation | 115
waiting | 116

wakefulness | 117
wander | 118
way | 119
weave | 120
whole | 121
wisdom | 122
wonder | 123
yearning | 124
yield | 125
zeal | 126

ABOUT THE AUTHOR | 127

Preface

THERE IS MUCH IN life that does not work out as we expected. There are headwinds, difficulties, and failures.

It is easy, therefore, to be disappointed. And for some, disappointment coalesces into bitterness or despair.

But there are other possibilities. Headwinds may strengthen our resolve. Failures may cause us to re-evaluate. Despair may lead to conversion and transformation.

When all else fails, there is poetry. Beauty remains. One only needs to look. But one may need new eyes.

And new eyes don't come easily. Certainly not when fair winds blow and all seems well. Instead, new eyes are often the product of pain or loss. But they may also emerge in times of contemplation and reflection. In these, and possibly other circumstances, a new way of seeing things is hardly the fruit of our own prowess. More likely, they are a gift sourced by the enlightening spirit. And that dynamic remains largely in the realm of mystery.

Much more, of course, could and should be said. But let poetry do the talking. It is a language all by itself. It has its own clarity masked in opaqueness. It may well let beauty shine.

When all else fails—and much does—there is poetry.

Charles Ringma
Brisbane, Australia
2021

achieve

it never begins with achievement.

the pressure to think and function like this, is misplaced.

achievement has a different genesis.

there is first gift,

and the dream,

and the struggle,

and being denuded.

and what we achieve is often different to what we had hoped.

so, we achieve gropingly

and with a chastened hope.

wonderment comes with such surprising outcomes.

act

life is not an act

on a stage.

one can't keep up such a performance.

weariness will grasp us

like a winter chill.

life is

an immersion,

a baptism.

it is a sacrament

that knows

the movement of blessedness, death, and resurrection.

agency

in the bigger scheme

of things

and in life's institutional complexities,

we can feel, o, so small,

so overwhelmed,

so powerless.

but

act we can and must.

doing even the smallest of things.

a meal for the yet unknown neighbour.

answer

the very nature of our existence

is a demanding and persistent question.

and the whole of life is a groping and stumbling answer.

while certain of the answers

in our youth,

in aging,

our answers are often fragile and ambiguous,

but possibly more painfully real?

anticipation

what we have hoped for

may well happen.

it may also elude us.

and it may depend

on the preparation

we have so lovingly expended

and the forethought we have ever so carefully contributed.

to anticipate

is not simply to wait,

but to *act* in hope.

anxiety

like a cattle-brand

anxiety is seared into the flesh of our humanity.

the strong are anxious

about what they may lose.

the poor are anxious

about what they need.

the faithful

are anxious about their failings.

and the dying

are not quite sure what awaits them.

art

in concentration camps

music groups are formed.

in prisons

artists discover their vocation.

in dictatorships

street-art becomes prophetic.

a revolutionary vision may well begin with the artist,

rather than the activist.

beauty

it was a bleak day.

discouragement ruled my heart.

the beach was windswept.

the waves turbulent with its white and angry froth.

the brahminy kite drifted in the wind,

its golden-brown wings colouring the grey landscape.

it suddenly turned

and landed close to where i stood, captivated.

it eyed me ever so carefully.

beauty had come to earth

and to my heart.

becoming

in the enfolding

of love and encouragement,

one's life unfolds

like a ripple in a pond.

it matters little

whether the pond is deep or shallow.

the ripples are there

when one throws oneself into its murky blackness.

being

in becoming

is one's being.

in doing

is one's becoming.

and in waiting,

crying,

and praying,

one's being is shaped

not in human prowess,

but in a vulnerability

of humility and joy.

commitment

however unsure and reluctant

we may be,

we do need to make painful choices,

and commit

ourselves to tasks,

whose outcomes may remain shaded

in a blanket of uncertainty.

never mind, don't become immobile!

dare to act!

communion

this wonderful dynamic

is not limited

to the religious sphere,

but may well be

our deepest human experience.

we may commune

with nature,

our inner being,

with others,

and with the brooding and life-giving spirit.

as such,

it is a gift and a way of life.

compromise

of course

we all want to hold the high ground,

and that our way

is right and just.

but in the blinding light

of a brutal honesty

we too

will have to admit

that we also are implicated in failure and wrong-doing.

none of us

has clean hands.

thus,

forgiveness has to find its way to all of us.

consolation

our very individuality

is the mark

of our greatest loneliness.

who really knows us?

and who can bring comfort?

lover, family, and friends

can only touch the edges of our ways,

our very being eludes them.

only the dove,

the hovering spirit,

can bring us consolation,

and who can anticipate its appearing?

contentment

it is but momentary.

the fragments of an already broken shard.

it is water running

through one's fingers.

it is gone before it is grasped.

better to hold to longing

than to wait for contentment.

better to expect

the surprise

than to hope for what cannot be orchestrated.

control

whether its source is

familial, spiritual, institutional, or political,

oppression

rankles the human spirit,

and evokes the cry of pain

and acts of protest,

even in the face of the greatest odds.

but

do *resist* the seemingly irresistible!

convenience

we may all too readily see ourselves

as principled

and committed to our causes.

but

convenience beckons us

like a forbidden lover.

it is wearisome

to do what is right,

and the easy road opens so unexpectedly

before us.

how do we face this smiling seducer?

curiosity

of course,

we would like to think

that curiosity lies within us.

but

it lies elsewhere.

it is evoked by

the babbling brook,

the gurgling baby,

the wistful look,

the shrouded mountain top,

the speaker's enigmatic saying,

and the strange and haunting icon.

let these lead you to the pathways of imagination.

dabble

mastery,

professionalism,

and expertise

are the markers of success.

but

time to dabble,

to stare out of the window,

to let things fall,

may well be the fount of a new inspiration.

doubt

once, i was so sure

of most things

in my ever-so-tiny domain.

but

in the greater scheme of things

more questions, rather than answers,

have become my necessary

but troubling companions.

i welcome them now.

duty

i want freedom,

but

duty also calls me.

it's persistent inner voice

reminds me

that true freedom

is not simply freedom *from,* but freedom *for.*

energy

of course

energy has to do with physical dynamics.

but

when new possibilities

charged by hopefulness

emerge,

almost anything is possible.

enlightenment

surprisingly

this gift

is bathed in blindness.

it is only

much, much, later

that one recognises

that new insights have emerged.

thus,

enlightenment is the gift of hindsight.

envy

cain was envious of abel

and killed him.

envy

is generic, but always parasitic.

it has a victim mentality,

cloaked in a coagulated self-pity,

with its refrain: "why the other, and not me."

it's antidote

is the gentle gift of gratitude.

faith

it seems

that we have a perennial need

to believe in someone or something.

faith can thus inspire us,

motivate us,

and call forth our greatest commitments.

but

faith can also lead us astray.

history is replete with false messiahs

in whom

we placed our fervent and foolish trust.

fate

we are deeply troubled and perplexed

when misfortunes

are repeated in family and other social systems.

were these things just meant to be?

are mistakes repeatable?

are there deeper forces at work

beyond our knowing and doing?

these questions will seldom be answered satisfactorily,

and won't ever go away.

fear

there is a fear

that paralyses us.

there is also a fear

that galvanises us.

it need not be a manacle that binds,

but

an open door

that moves us forward.

fecundity

the dark density of the tropical rain forest.

the restless waves of seemingly endless barley fields.

the wooing of a lover.

a nurse's care in an i.c.u. ward.

the ever-attentiveness of one's friend.

the luscious redness of tomatoes.

but

despite so much goodness,

and so much that is given,

in often ungrateful hands,

the heart aches for the many who still live in such barren places.

gaze

we move too quickly

through each day.

hurried and hassled.

sometimes frantic.

mesmerised by much-doing and much-having

we lose ourselves.

slow down.

gaze.

be renewed by wonderment!

gentleness

our modern way of life

is marked by

assertion,

competitiveness,

and power *over* others.

find a new path.

walk

in the way of gentleness,

sharing,

consensus building,

and community.

generosity

to be generous

with your time and resources

is not an act

of self-diminishment,

but

of self-enhancement.

gift

there is the gift of

life.

the gift of the

earth.

the gifts

of family, friendship, and community.

and the gifts

of nurture, education, work, and creativity.

so much is

given.

there is so much room for gratitude and celebration.

gratitude

is the music of

the soul.

the joy of

the goodness of others.

the melody

that overflows to others.

help

some find it, o, so difficult

to ask for help and assistance.

others, sadly, expect everything

from someone else.

but

the need for the help of others

knocks on all of our doors.

and

to assist someone else, is a call that comes to each of us.

holding

there are things we need

to hold on to.

and there are things we need

to let go.

even good things

we may need to relinquish.

this is possible.

we can do this,

as long as we are held in love.

hope

even when all seems lost

hope can arise

like the phoenix out of ashes and decay.

its surprising power

lies not so much in waiting for something to happen,

but

in actively participating in the very things hoped for.

hospitality

in the very beginning

there was not

duty and work,

but hospitality.

welcome to life!

welcome to the earth!

welcome to community!

there was hospitality,

and then there was responsibility.

hurt

hurt comes to all of us.

we wound and disappoint others,

and others sin against us.

thus,

reconciliation and healing

are humanity's greatest calling,

even greater than empire-building.

interruption

i am ever so guilty

of being committed to tasks,

rather than creating space

for conversation,

dialogue,

and relationships.

if only

i had known

the blessedness

of putting to one side

what i foolishly thought was so important.

insight

i thought i had understood,

but

i later realised that what was really said

had eluded me.

that

was already an insight.

joy

while happiness

is often a self-creation,

joy

is the surprise

that springs from the wells

of gratitude.

justice

often wrapped

in a cloak

of what is fair *for* me,

justice

trumpets a different melody.

what is just

for all,

irrespective of who they are,

is the choral melody.

let it ring out loud and clear in our broken world!

lament

loss and tragedy

can entomb us.

and our very silence

can fracture the membranes of

a broken heart.

instead,

cry out,

pour out your grief, disappointments, and questions.

and in the lull that follows

hear afresh the murmurs of your heart.

limitation

we are neither

the gods, fates, and powers of human existence.

and though

we foolishly think that we can do much,

we are merely a whisper

and sometimes only a whimper.

but

that may be the seedbed of the good that will come.

listless

out of my routine.

in uncertain times.

in-between one thing and another.

in a time of waiting.

in reoccurring dreams.

this inner turmoil and listlessness

nudges me

like a thorn in my foot.

its disturbing presence may be a herald.

liturgy

every form of public worship

is liturgy.

a football grand-final,

a mass protest,

a political movement,

can all be acts of worship.

thus,

liturgy belongs to life,

not only to the sanctuary.

but,

who and what should we worship?

luminous

a raindrop on a petal.

a sunrise breaking through the clouds.

the joyful cry of a child.

a remark from a friend.

the touch of a lover.

an unexpected insight.

everywhere,

life shines,

despite its shadows.

maintenance

there is

a restlessness

in the human spirit

that leads to ever new adventures and projects.

but

there is also the challenge

to do the ordinary and necessary things.

these too

are to be seen as noble and good.

manifestation

we observe

and seek to understand

all that is around us.

what beauty!

yet so much is still shrouded in mystery.

but

sometimes things become wonderfully clear.

a revelation!

we are struck not by a hand, but by a whisper.

maturity

while its signs may be

full development and wisdom,

and may suggest

strength and dependability,

ours is but a flawed maturity.

we are only ever on the way, and much still eludes us.

memory

anything can be a trigger.

and in every way

we may wander into this great storehouse.

unlike a carefully organised museum,

the storehouse of memory,

is ever reappropriated,

and nothing is ever quite the same.

its very creativity,

can nurture,

an earth-shattering relevance.

mending

my female forebears

mended their clothes and darned their woollen socks,

usually in the evening

in front of the fire,

while the men smoked their pipes.

a nostalgic image.

but

the gentle art of mending belongs to all of us.

more than socks,

relationships and communities

need mending as well.

mentoring

so many

so alone

in the journey of life.

where are

the women and men of wisdom,

who give of themselves

in the gentle art

of the formation of others?

since we are not self-made

companions on the journey are to be welcomed.

mercy

in the rwandan, south african, and cambodian

atrocities

men and women of courage

extended

forgiveness and mercy

to each other.

surely, we can do the same

for our often petty and banal stupidities?

midwifery

a career for some

in hospital and home settings.

but

a calling for all of us

to bring forth

the most delicate dreams.

monotone

o, how we love

our tribalism

with its oft-repeated but untested certainties.

the group

with its web of loyalties.

but

wisdom is not a monotone.

it is a symphony.

and

in the face of the other

a fuller understanding is born.

mourning

a loved one

has passed away.

a dream

has been shattered.

plans

did not come to fruition.

mourning

is with us.

but

so is the morning.

a new day appears.

mystical

there are many ways of

knowing

and seeing.

the mystical

need not be the sole domain of gurus and monks.

inspiration

knocks at every door.

open the door, just a little!

naming

in naming a child

we are not providing a badge or a label.

we are expressing a hope.

naming

not only identifies something,

but

celebrates a future.

narrators

it is not so much

that we all tell stories.

but

our very life is a story

for good or ill.

thus, we all have something to say.

and when it is a lived narrative, it is very loud!

neighbour

in our crowded world

we have lost

the neighbour.

to find him or her

may well be

to find a truer version of ourselves.

neophyte

like a young, newly planted shrub

we

are only ever

beginners

in the tapestry of life.

who knows

what we may yet blossom into?

but make sure we are deeply rooted!

nestle

a babe

at a mother's breast.

an orchid

in the branch of a forest gum.

a lover

in a caring embrace.

but

we can all nestle in

to our homes,

friendships,

and in the brooding spirit.

nutritive

nurture

is not limited to childhood.

we all need

care,

encouragement,

affirmation,

and the gentlest of love.

occupation

generic to the human condition

is the call to work.

we are *homo faber*.

but

we are so much more than our occupations.

don't let work wholly define you!

also be

muse,

dreamer,

lover.

ode

we are

really

a song,

an orchestration.

and we are this most clearly

as a symphony.

o, the beauty

of many voices and instruments.

may our despondent world

be renewed

by tuneful harmonies!

omission

of course

we do what is good, but also what is unacceptable.

such mixed-up creatures that we are!

but

the greater challenge

is to do what we must.

so often

we neglect what lies close at hand.

opportunity

what are we?

perpetrators of the familiar

or

readers of the signs of the times,

who see the openings,

hear the new melody,

anticipate

what has not entered into the dreams of others.

orchestrate

yes,

i have met them.

they are not the organisational leaders,

nor are they in the limelight

garnering kudos for themselves.

they

work behind the scenes,

they have the ideas,

they make things happen in concert with others.

o, how silently they suffer.

ought

o, so weighty.

and

often so burdensome

coming from oppressive places.

but

there are things we should do,

places we need to protect,

situations we need to enhance,

people we should nurture.

ought

can be the banks in which the river of life flows.

outlier

most of us

are centrally located

in the many institutions of our social landscape.

maintenance and continuity

are the oft refrain.

but

we also need outliers,

those on the margins,

those with different perspectives

to break the mold.

don't wish for such a calling! you will suffer!

overflow

a river needs its source.

an activity needs its conceptualisation.

a vision needs its inspiration.

love needs its inner resources.

so much of life

is the overflow

of what is usually hidden in the deep recesses of the human spirit.

paradox

there are those

who see everything in straight lines.

but

life has its ambiguities.

and

more basically

we are even a paradox to ourselves.

pardon

there are those

who live with a sense of entitlement.

and

it is easy for us to be self-righteous.

but

we all fail,

particularly in relation to the distant neighbour.

to be pardoned and forgiven can put us on the road to recovery.

paschal

i had a dream.

it would not leave me.

i put it into action.

it died prematurely.

i all but gave it up.

but

a new door opened.

the paschal mystery swam into view.

patience

patience is not

being patient with what interests *me*.

patience

is being patient with the other,

who not only does not interest me,

but

annoys and frustrates me.

i am clearly not patient.

perseverance

it is one thing

to persist in what is pleasurable

and expedient.

it is quite another thing

to persevere

with what is difficult.

o, how easily we abandon

the long road of justice and peacemaking!

precarious

for the powerful

life is about control.

for others

life is vulnerable and precarious.

but

all face unexpected headwinds

and

all need to be flexible, persevering, and prayerful.

prelude

this life

is not a prelude

to a future life.

this life is what we have,

however precarious, beautiful, or difficult.

what lies beyond

remains in the meanderings of faith.

provoke

of course

we are to be gentle,

cooperative,

and committed to community building.

but

there are times

where we need to be provocative

especially

when what we love

is threatened by stupidities.

radical

it's the often pretentious label

of those seeking to bring about change.

but

so often

they give up

and revert to old ways of thinking and acting.

a radical

surely

is one who has gone through and continues in the deepest

purgation.

rapine

we

should have cared,

nurtured,

and protected.

instead,

we have plundered

other nations and communities

and

the earth that so generously sustains us.

blood is on our hands.

is there a fountain pure and deep enough where we can be

purged?

ready

weeks before the beginning of a new school semester,

i would dream,

always late and unprepared.

are we ever ready?

maybe, for some events?

but

never for life itself.

it is full of the unexpected.

reciprocity

a value

that was part of an older world.

now

it is demand

and

i will take.

and as a result,

we continue to diminish ourselves

and tarnish the ever-so-delicate social fabric.

renew

there is much that can't be renewed.

i can't renew my youthful fitness in old age.

and

long-fractured relationships

are often not restored.

but

i can renew

my saddened inner being

with the gift of forgiveness.

reprieve

usually, a stay of execution

extended to a condemned person.

but

we need to extend this to ourselves.

under societal and our own pressures and demands,

we overextend ourselves resulting in ill-health and depression.

give

yourself a reprieve!

restore

o, the promises of

restoration,

renewal,

recovery.

but

so much remains broken.

we are always torn between hope and disappointment.

return

no matter

how far we travel

in the journey of forgetfulness

regarding both the good and the bad,

the return

always beckons us.

to the good, a renewed gratitude.

to the bad, the pursuit of reconciliation.

risk

with certitude

lies continuity.

with growth

lies pain and transformation.

with risk

the unknown pathway of hope.

routine

with

a natural disaster,

a pandemic,

war,

ill health,

our routines are fractured

and often dissipated.

routines are important.

rebuild them in new and creative ways!

sabbath

winter's snow lies deep.

the earth sleeps.

our busy day lies heavy.

we sleep a dreamless slumber.

work and rest,

day and night,

spring and winter,

the magic pattern of recovery.

build this pattern into the fabric of your life!

sacramental

is

there

magic in the ordinary?

work is toil,

but

it can also be

the beauty of begetting

and bringing the new into being.

sacrifice

this

noble move

of self-giving for the sake of the other,

costing us much,

is

often frittered away by the recipient.

sacrifice

is so often the lonely and thankless journey.

satyagraha

working for real change

is no frivolous

and superficial undertaking.

it is

truth-obstinacy

capable

of the greatest commitment and sacrifice.

search

the

greatest search

is not

to know what you are looking for.

the

greater search

is to find the unknowable.

shadow

it is

the refraction of light

that causes the shadow.

and it is

the light of enlightenment

and its painful truth

that causes us

to face our own shadow-side.

tapestry

we

are a story

not a single line.

we

are a tapestry

not a single thread.

and

neither the story nor the tapestry

is yet complete.

tension

life

is not a nice equilibrium.

it is

dynamic,

and full of tension and challenges.

welcome this!

it opens such opportunities

for

painful growth.

test

you

can test yourself

to see

if you are reaching your goals.

but

responding

to life's unexpected challenges

is the greater test.

we may well fall,

only to rise again.

thankfulness

it is not true

that everything is our own achievement.

much

has been given by others.

often

in unexpected ways.

being thankful

is being your best and truest self.

threshold

have you ever

stood excitedly

on the edge

of a

new love,

adventure,

discovery?

you may pause at the threshold – but the new beckons you!

trace

much-having

is not

our deepest longing.

but

significance is.

we want to leave a trace

in offspring,

writings,

art,

discoveries.

a small sign of our questing for the eternal!

transition

when

earthquakes, wars, pandemics, tragedies

crash into our lives,

we

are up-ended

and find ourselves in transitional spaces.

marked by uncertainty

we haltingly try to find our way.

it beckons us!

twilight

i love

the sun's mellow and dreamy

descent

at day's end.

it's like a big sigh.

it's enough

of all we have sought to do.

and

an invitation to think about what could have been

but

was not.

unbearable

we

are not

as strong, brave, and compassionate

as we would like to be.

too much

of life's difficulties and injustices

are more than we can bear.

who will uphold us?

uncertain

we are not

as sure-footed as mountain goats.

often

ours is an uncertain stride.

but

we walk ahead.

underestimate

we

are more

than what we think we are.

much

lies hidden

in the caverns of our fears

and insecurities.

but

the cave's mouth lies open!

understory

the towering

mountain ash tree

reaches for the sky.

great women and men

leave their mark on history.

but

most of us

are the understory.

readily forgotten, but important nonetheless.

unguarded

no matter

how careful we may seek to be,

we are never

totally safeguarded.

we are

all vulnerable.

and

anything can come our way.

unity

a great ideal

and

a dangerous notion

when

cast in the garb of uniformity.

far healthier

the difficult dynamic of unity and diversity.

unknowing

to come to this

is a great break-through,

for

we seldom acknowledge

what we don't know.

but

it is the gateway

to new possibilities.

utopia

o, the dream

of

messianic charlatans.

heaven on earth.

what bliss.

but

what violence and manipulation

lies at the heart

of what seems to be so wonderful.

verdant

everywhere

the images of parched land.

and then

the long-awaited flash-floods.

o,

the wonder of the greenest green.

this landscape

is at times our soulscape.

vicarious

there

are times

in our vulnerable existence

when someone else

has to be there for us,

to carry us,

to act on our behalf.

allow yourself to be carried!

visitation

o, yes,

sometimes,

and unexpectedly,

we feel

that someone or something has drawn close.

a door now stands open.

the blockage has disappeared.

an inner renewal

has begun to resonate

in a previously discouraged heart.

waiting

i know the pain

of waiting

for something

that is so desirable and good.

i am still waiting.

rationalisations don't give me answers.

i am still waiting

but

with a deeply chastened hope.

wakefulness

like the monks

i usually wake around 3am.

i am fully awake

and the most productive thoughts come.

they order the rest of the day.

wakefulness is inspirational

and the fountain of attentiveness.

wander

o, yes,

we were told

to stay on well-trodden paths

to be safe.

but

we are safer for having wandered.

we

may have found what we were looking for.

way

there is a way

that

I must walk.

since

i heard the call

deep within my being.

others have not understood.

its way has been a lonely road.

weave

many colourful threads.

great patience.

an emerging design.

so

it is in community building.

its beauty may even startle us!

whole

so desired.

but

so ungraspable.

and

so delusional and dangerous.

our ideologies, dictatorships, and utopias,

are the wrecks of history,

like rusting tanks,

in the egyptian desert.

wisdom

a rare fragrance

and

ever so delicate.

it

is not possessed.

it

appears

in a chastened heart.

wonder

when

it disappears from life

we taste dust in our mouths.

when

it appears

everything is ablaze with light.

yearning

it

is a pain

that goes beyond

all boundaries.

it is profligate, expansive, unstoppable.

when

shaped by goodness

it can bring about a new world.

yield

is

life about self-assertion?

is it

about domination?

or

is life a dance

where we move forward,

move together,

and give way?

zeal

to be zealous

is to be

overcome with passion and concern,

and

dangerously close to over-reach.

zeal

needs to become tempered iron.

About the author

Charles Ringma is an academic who has worked with the marginalised. He has lived in intentional community. He has worked in cross-cultural settings. He is concerned about justice issues and plants rain-forest trees. He is a Franciscan tertiary (*tssf*). His previous books in this genre are *Ragged Edges, Sabbath Time, Chase Two Horses,* and *With Your Latte.* Check out charlesringma.com and holyscribblers.blogspot.com

www.ingramcontent.com/pod-product-compliance
Lightning Source LLC
Chambersburg PA
CBHW070500100426
42743CB00010B/1698